Guernica, revisited

Guernica
revisited

poems

richard vargas

Press 53
Winston-Salem

Press 53, LLC
PO Box 30314
Winston-Salem, NC 27130

First Edition

Silver Concho Poetry Series
edited by Pamela Uschuk and William Pitt Root

Copyright © 2014 by Richard Vargas

All rights reserved, including the right of reproduction in whole or in part in any form except in the case of brief quotations embodied in critical articles or reviews. For permission, contact author at editor@Press53.com, or at the address above.

Cover design by Kevin Morgan Watson

Cover art, "MQ-9/Predator" Copyright © 2011 by Mahwish Chishty, used by permission of the artist.

Author photo by Lisa Blackmer

Printed on acid-free paper
ISBN 978-1-941209-03-5

For Lisa, with love…
here's looking at you, kid.

Acknowledgments

The author would like to acknowledge the following publications in which some of these poems were previously published, sometimes in a slightly different form: *Adobe Walls, Big Hammer, BorderSenses, Camas, Chiron Review, Cultural Weekly, Cutthroat, DoveTales, Drunken Boat, Kweli, Malpaís Review, Mezcla, Naugatuck River Review, phati'tude, Rattle, Smithsonian Dia de los Muertos Literary Series, The Más Tequila Review,* and *Xispas*.

Guernica, revisited

Foreword by E. A. "Tony" Mares	xi
the end of Superman	1
the road taken	3
for a friend who objects to comparing the events leading up to the Holocaust with what is happening today in Arizona	5
déjà vu	7
song for Shenandoah	8
with friends like these	15
villain, rebooted	16
field of vision	18
when you beat me	19
what war?	20
Guernica, revisited	22
not a medal, but a poem	23
we could be heroes	24
the night Nixon landed in China	26
strange fruit	27
Marilyn	28
a sin to remember	29
a birthday wish for a friend	30
why i feed the birds	32
smoking outside in the alley at 3 a.m.	33
the origami master's wife speaks	34
i have Sandra's boots	35
father's day poem	36
childhood's end	37
i wouldn't wish this one on anybody	39
death in the afternoon	40
living and dying; a Westside poem	41
the Governor abolishes the death penalty	43
why my ex-wife will go to heaven	44
women and guns	46
we go boom… after Patti Smith's cover of "My Generation"	47
the company provides a free lunch on the day it lays off 250 employees	48
no hard feelings	50

a goodbye	51
last day / final exit	53
the temp	54
almost bottom	55
no regrets	56
two-coyote day at Rinconada Canyon	58
milagro #1	59
milagro #2	60
milagro #3	61
milagro #4	62
waking up	63
sea turtle swimming to L.A.	64
lowered expectations	66
a Thanksgiving poem	67
Sonny style	68
i dream	69
i dream of tongues	70
i dream about remembering to forget	71
city of the lost	72
milagro #7	73
milagro #10	74
wedding poem for Lily and Chris	75
bed bug love	77
milagro #12	78
milagro #13	79
milagro #14	80
milagro #16	82
milagro #17	83
salvation	84
fifty-something	86
something to look forward to	87
funeral song	88
final words	89

Foreword

by
E. A. "Tony" Mares

If I had to describe in one sentence an over-arching quality of *Guernica, revisited*, it would be as follows: "*Guernica, revisited* is one of the best contemporary expressions of human compassion within the domain of poetry I have ever read." I do not write this sentence casually. For here we encounter a profound identification of the poet with his suffering, struggling, tragic, and at times playful, funny, and entertaining fellow *Homo sapiens*.

While it is not unusual for a poet in these times to be engaged in the struggles for social justice and human dignity, it is, I believe, unusual to find that social concern expressed in such intensely personal, concrete terms as in these poems that arise from lived experience and a careful development of poetic craftsmanship. Richard Vargas is a member of the "boomer" generation. He acknowledges this, and in a brilliant poem "we go boom… after Patti Smith's cover of 'My Generation,'" he brings out the dark side of a wantonly consumer-oriented society. In the final stanzas he writes: "this is mine/that's mine/those will/be mine//they call us boomers/watch us go boom/they call us boomers//boom/Boom/BOOM."

If he takes the scalpel to his own generation, Richard Vargas does so while at the same time exploring with a directness that still manages to have heart, the inhumane aspects of an exploitative economic system. In a series of poems, "the company provides a free lunch on the day it lays off 250 employees," "no hard feelings," "a goodbye," and "last day/final exit," the issue of unemployment becomes very personal. In these poems, and in several that follow, there is no hollow ranting or rhetoric about oppression or "the system," rather there is a stark presentation of an overpowering reality that says, "this is the world, our world, as it is now, as it exists now." It is a world we see every time we look in the mirror. As we look into that mirror, Richard Vargas also tries to help us see it doesn't have to be this way. There is always hope we can be better than we are most of the time.

While he captures the psychological terror of the unemployed in poems such as "*no regrets,*" and the bitter ironies of racism, immigration hypocrisy, and the daily insults suffered by the poor, in poems such as the magnificent "Song for Shenandoah," Vargas does not slip into a smug self-righteousness. Rather, he includes himself as afflicted as any with the human condition. I would not call this a volume of movement poetry, but when he raises social issues, he hits very hard. Hard, yes, and with a deep identification with all who are truly oppressed by a greedy economic system. My favorite of these poems is "the road taken," where the poet envisions an America where white racism has triumphed, minorities have been deported, and with the labor force gone, the country withers away until "all that remained/in the United States/of America besides/the angry the old/and the white/were a bunch of dried up/golf courses and an/ abundance of vacant/Walmarts/." At this point, the Mexicans "decided it was safe to return/with their lawnmowers/paint brushes/bags of cement/ mops and buckets/," because "the country was a bigger mess/than ever before and once again/there was plenty of work/for everyone."

There is a fine thread of eroticism running through many of these poems, such as in "strange fruit," where a lover offers a fig to "his mouth, teased his reluctant tongue, the taste/of its sweet red meat went down easy like/oysters, he licked his lips, asked her for more." As another example, there is "milagro #2" that rejoices in the four strawberries his lover has left for him on the kitchen counter. Vargas writes "and when I bite one/its juice squirts on/my tongue sweet/like a woman's kiss/that says yes/yes and/yes." And then there is the exquisite "milagro #4" where, in the midst of planting a lush garden, the poet sees the woman as "my little goddess/of the earth/grower of things/hot and sweet//my life is full/ of flavor//because of you."

Deep, also, is a moral outrage at how we treat each other. At the same time, this moral stance is not preachy and it is moderated by a quiet sense of humor that inhabits so many of these poems. Vargas is well aware of how modern corporate society tries, and often succeeds, to diminish us as individuals, to make us feel our insignificance in relation to the giant engine of run-away capitalism. Yet he treats this theme with a quiet and sad sense of humor as in the poem "the end of Superman." In this fine poem, we as readers can so readily find empathy with a Superman who is, after all, an "illegal alien," the legally correct words yet code for the racists in our midst. Exposed as an "illegal alien," "Superman had nothing to say/and after the show turned/himself in to the nearest/ICE detention center/where he now sits with/the other detainees//becoming invisible/fading away."

Foreword

Over all, there is a serene quality to these poems. There is a pervading quietness. The poems never scream at you, even when they show the depravities of our time. I think this quietness derives from Richard Vargas' keen awareness of and appreciation for nature. For example, in "milagro #1," he sees green nopales covered with melting snow as "bejeweling pointed/spines with pearls/fallen from the sky."

It is impossible, I believe, to read these poems and not come away with the awareness that a powerful contemporary poetic voice has squarely faced himself and his times. He has looked unflinchingly into the mirror of his time and place in history and like Picasso with Guernica; he has seen there is no art, no beauty in our destructiveness. Yet there is a sliver of hope. And humor to carry us over the bombed out traumas of our world and our lives within that world. This is strong stuff. Strong poetry.

the end of Superman

no
it wasn't some devious plot
put into action by his nemesis
the pesky Lex Luthor
or a stray meteor shower
of that lethal poison
Green Kryptonite

it happened on
the Larry King show
during an interview
someone called in
wanted his opinion
on how to rid the
country of all the
lazy dirty illegals
invading the good
ol' U.S.A. and why
hadn't he done some-
thing about it already

Superman hemmed
and hawed saying
he didn't think it was
a legitimate threat
to national security
and besides from
an economic standpoint
it made no sense
and people everywhere
have a right to pursue
a better way of life
since borders don't
detract from the
fact that we're all

human beings with
the same wants
and needs

the caller spoke again
this time sounding a lot
like Glenn Beck until he
cleared his throat to
lower his voice as he
asked Superman why
he was going soft on
criminals and that
maybe he wasn't our
protector of truth
justice and the
American way
after all

Superman tried to
get a word in but then
the caller did the unexpected
he asked Superman to prove
his citizenship and by the way
wasn't he from another planet
which would truly make him
an illegal alien if there ever
was one

Superman had nothing to say
and after the show turned
himself in to the nearest
ICE detention center
where he now sits with
the other detainees

becoming invisible
fading away

the road taken

they had seen this before
the name-calling
the pointing of fingers
the feverish waving of
the flag and signs
telling them to
go home

so they did
where they watched
us look for new reasons
to blame for the fall
of our empire while
the roads crumbled
the bridges sagged and
collapsed as weeds
pushed through
the many cracks
in the pavement

they heard us cry
while our crops rotted
in the fields because we
had become too lazy
and soft to pick our
own lettuce and grapes
strawberries and onions

they shook their heads
when we started fighting
amongst ourselves
the clouds of acrid smoke
and the sound of gunfire
floated over the razored wire
wall and that invisible line
in the dirt we once
patrolled diligently
with flying drones and
neo-Nazi patriots

then the walls of inclusion
became the great walls
of exclusion as all
the brown people
were kicked out
then the black people
soon followed by anyone
deemed to be not white
enough to stay behind
last but not least were
God's chosen people
befuddled and confused
because they thought they
had finally passed over
to the right side of the
color line

then all that remained
in the United States
of America besides
the angry the old
and the white
were a bunch of dried up
golf courses and an
abundance of vacant
Walmarts

it was then that they
decided it was safe to return
with their lawnmowers
paint brushes
bags of cement
mops and buckets

the country was a bigger mess
than before and once again
there was plenty of work
for everyone

to a friend who objects to comparing the events leading up to the Holocaust with what is happening today in Arizona

for you "never again"
is personal and sacred
never again reduced
to less than human
never again to madmen
who spit their words
at you like careless
but calculated grenades
never again to being
scapegoat while a
government dulls
the minds and hearts
of its citizens to accept
the atrocities it will do
in their names

but even as i read this
we both know
it is happening again
all over the world
and right now within
our own borders

the tribes are different
yet they are the same
the raging wall of flame
that almost consumed
your people still burns
aided by strong winds
flapping the flags of old
and new hatreds

it's a modern day
pogrom in the making
fingers pointing at "illegal
aliens" and "anchor babies"
words devised to strip
away humanity from
the powerless

but you and i know
what's really going on
as i write this poem
as you read this poem
the names of brown people
are being redacted
from our children's
history books
the names of brown people
boxed up and banned
from our children's
classrooms

we both know this beginning
this beginning with an end
no one wants to think about
but dwells deep inside our
fear gnawing nonstop like
a shiny slick maggot

so let us use your words
your gift to the world
language to name
the unspeakable
the unimaginable
the horrible

we will stand together
shout them out with
your same passion
and defiance in the
face of this heartless
beast

never again
never again
nunca más

déjà vu

The mayor comes over to my table and says I am invited to join him and *el jefe* ICE agent for a drink. I walk over and sit down as the mayor pulls out a small black book and hands it to the agent. He begins to read aloud:

Richard Vargas, born in Compton, California. Members of your family came here from Mexico, and you are one generation removed from picking grapes and cotton. You went to school, the university, and now call yourself a "poet." We know that you masturbated incessantly in the 7th grade, and that you smoked pot on a daily basis when you were in college. You left California, but we still haven't found out why. You have a weakness for women, cigars, and expensive cognacs. Tell me, are you one of those hopeless romantics who refuses to accept the establishment of a Fourth Reich in your beloved United States?

"Well, some parts of the U.S. look like they beat you to the punch. But if you're asking me, there are certain neighborhoods in Albuquerque I wouldn't advise you to invade."

song for Shenandoah

for Luis Ramirez

The Devil has the people by the throat…
—Annina, explaining to Rick why she is
leaving her country, *Casablanca*

I.
oh Shenandoah, strip mined and bare
by the sweat of men cursing in broken
English as coal-black dust streaks their
European faces with eyes on the
look-but-don't-touch prize

mother to Tommy and Jimmy
Dorsey who gave our soldiers
big band swing music as they
dodged bullets on the way to
victory over Berlin and Tokyo

land of Mrs. T's Pierogies
and a meager slice of the
American dream worth
$12, 562 per capita income
at the start of the 21st century

Shenandoah
some say the name
Shenandoah
is derived from indigenous tongues
Shenandoah
means "beautiful star daughter"

II.
small town once proud once
thriving thirty thousand strong
today's headcount barely five thousand
Shenandoah hangs on like another
forgotten whistle stop crying out
for new blood new people
until we heed your call

we climb your walls and
wade through muddy brown river
we walk and run across deserts
hide in bushes and seek shade
while drinking warm water from
discarded plastic Coke bottles
tied to our waists with twine

we die with swollen tongues from border heat
we smother in the trunks of cars and asphyxiate
packed like sardines in 40 ft. trailers left to
bake in the noonday sun for the jobs you
don't want and the wages you refuse

III.
the grass will always be greener
the grass will always be greener
the grass will always be greener

Shenandoah, we claim you
cut your lawns
bus the tables
wash your dishes
take out the garbage
sweep your sidewalks
shore up crumbling walls
patch the cracks in your
weathered face with flowers
that bloom in the spring

Om-pah-pah
Om-pah-pah
the bass of a tuba
vibrates dirty windows
shakes the dust off
worn and faded curtains
we bring *tortillas* and *pico
de gallo* to your table
Tecate and *pan dulce*
the laughter of children
breaking open Spider-Man
piñatas on birthdays
we are grateful because
for us a day's hard work
is a gift from God

IV.
Shenandoah, your children walk
the streets angry and drunk on
the sweet lies of corporate media
mouthpieces singing empty and false:
The Mexicans are coming!
The Mexicans are coming!
The Mexicans are here!

a man's head kicked hard
with the force of a hate unleashed
from the dark side of fear and loathing
will crack like a melon dropped
on the pavement and its juices
will slowly leak and stain the street

a religious medal hanging from
the neck and stomped into a man's
chest will imprint the holy face
of the savior deep into the skin
brand him in the name of
twisted salvation

Jesus salva
he convulses
Jesus salva
he foams at
the mouth
Jesus salva
he is still

hiding behind screen names
on the internet a new generation
of minutemen join in
take aim and post comments:
"these boys sacrificed their futures

in much the same way a marine
sacrifices his life on the battlefield
we are being invaded
if i was on the jury no way
these boys would be convicted
more dead illegals will discourage
future border jumps"

V.
sometimes a moment
is an hour, a week, a year
sometimes a decade or
a century passes in the blink
of an eye when all it takes
to recall the history of
our people buried deep
in our genes is the
sound of one word
wetback
is the humiliation of
tired and hungry ancestors
enduring its ugly sound
while picking Texas cotton
and California grapes from
sunup to sundown
wetback
is the mean reminder of
all that can never be and
all that will be denied
wetback
is the neighborhood
where houses can be rented
and the side of the railroad
tracks that are off limits
after dark
wetback
is long drives down
dusty roads looking
for crops to pick and ditches
to dig in a strange land
where wages are determined
by skin color

VI.
and still we come
again and again

Shenandoah, why are you weeping
why are your shoulders hung low
do not hide your face in shame
your sad cry rolling through
the valleys and bouncing off
the mountains is not in vain
no matter how many miles
there are between us
how many walls are raised
to keep us out

we are
coming home
coming home

coming home
to you

with friends like these

> *There comes a time when silence is betrayal.*
> —Dr. Martin Luther King, Jr.

why do you bite your tongue
until it bleeds strawberry red

turn your pretty white head while
targets are nailed to our backs

when we meet you talk about
the weather and your cats

keep it simple and sweet
don't worry be happy

what use to wallow in the shit-
storm that greets us every day

maybe you'll speak up when
they come to take me away

and maybe you won't
that being said

your golden silence is deadly
i scratch the shiny surface
find only words of lead

villain, rebooted

it happened after my ass got kicked for the umpteenth time
sent home with cuts and bruises
my colorful duds ragged and torn

sewing and mending, what they don't talk about when
you're given your super power
yech

so while licking my wounds, drinking a beer on the sofa
and catching up with the news on CNN, i had an epiphany
i almost felt stupid since it was staring me in the face
all this time
i decided to reinvent myself and aim for world domination
with a fresh approach
i traded in my skin tight bodysuit and cape for a nice navy
blue suit, bought off the rack, not tailor made
and a power tie for every day of the week
also ordered a shiny black pair of Florsheim
wingtips from Zappos.com
turned in my helmet for an
ivy league class ring
and the *pièce de résistance*

a small pin made in china
of the stars and stripes
displayed on my left lapel
right over where my heart
is supposed to be

now i can sleep at night knowing
 i'll never have to wash that damn spider webbing
out of my hair again and dodging razor sharp knives
projecting from a pair of fists has become a distant
memory

and my new super power?
i merely open my mouth and people gather around
anxious to believe whatever i say

what-ever-i-say

and this time i know
i can't lose

field of vision

bumper stickers leftover
from last presidential
campaign still cling
to rear window of my
fourteen-yr.-old Hyundai
proclaiming slogans
now empty like last week's
Madison Ave. marketing
schemes

they peel off easy
not as hard as i thought
wadded up they take
their place in the trashcan
next to discarded Slurpee
cups and other fast food
trash

i finish pumping
the gas and get in
behind the wheel
look in my rear-
view mirror

amazed at how much
more i can see

when you beat me

for Occupy

does your arm tire
as you swing your
baton into the thud
of my flesh and bone
and you hear me
moan in pain
when you crack
my ribs and jab
my soft belly
do you feel like a
job well done when
you pin me on the
ground and harness
my wrists like a
rodeo cowboy
hogties cattle

no matter that
we are both looked
down upon by those
on their balconies
of glass and steel
who laugh and joke
as they spread caviar
on fancy crackers
that will never pass
our lips

while you choke me
knock me down
look at how they
raise their flutes
of exquisite champagne
sparkling in the sun

blinding you with
cold brilliance
and empty nods
of approval

what war?

for A.J.

my *compa* calls to say his nineteen-yr.-old nephew
was the only survivor this morning
when the vehicle he was in was
blown apart by an IED somewhere
on an Afghani dirt road and i can vaguely
remember him as the little guy who
showed up at birthday parties and
family picnics on the 4th of July
trying to bust open the *piñata*
and running with the pack as
the kids played tag and climbed
the playground slide and swings
a little boy just like the rest

i wish i could recall something
specific like a scar or a dimple
then they all start flooding my memory
all the little boys who crossed
my path over the years and they
all look the same goddamnit
just like now in their camouflage
fatigues   boots   cap
even when i close my eyes
feel the wrinkles on my forehead
scrunch as i try hard to individualize
by name and year but they all
look alike as i tell him i'm sorry
i hope he's okay but then we
both are silent because
we know what that means
they will patch him up
send him back out for more
instead of home where he should be
chasing his dreams during the week
cruising for chicks on the weekend
doing what we did when we were nineteen

later i check the internet for news
but there is none to be found
it's all about the economy
healthcare and an old quarterback
hanging around for one more season
these men
these kids
dying on the other side of the world
aren't news anymore

i found a website where the number
of deaths for next month is already
projected

shame on us
for what we accept
shame on us
for what we
are willing
to forget

Guernica, revisited

the child is lying face down in the dirt, barefoot. his pants
are torn, exposing the backside of his leg, the skin's surface
dull with a layer of fine dust. head turned to the side, half
of the face is gone. hair is stiff, matted. he looks like a doll
someone just threw away. the family gathers around their
home where walls no longer stand and brick has been
pulverized into grit and debris burying their loved ones,
their belongings. a bed has been removed from the rubble;
under an old sleeping bag are the bodies of an adult and
two children. they look peaceful and asleep, huddled close
together for warmth. but they are not sleeping. overhead,
metallic raptors spread their wings with grace and ride
the high desert winds with ease, their cyber-cameras survey
the damage, send images half way around the globe where
men in starched uniforms focus on their military-issue
computer monitors, drink their morning coffee, take notes,
and fill out reports.

Picasso's ghost walks
among the carnage, weeping.
there is no art here.

not a medal, but a poem

brown desert children
dressed in their best clothes
chasing each other around
tables and chairs where the
wedding party sits surrounded
by family and friends
this day to celebrate and remember
turned to grief and shock with
a flash a boom a puff of smoke
a small shoe flying through the air

sitting in rooms on the other side of the globe
in the middle of another desert
uniformed video game junkies
finger their keyboards and
hi-tech joy sticks as words like
"alleged" and "probable" increase
the pressure of a thumb on a trigger button
until an innocent child obliterated
is written up as the equivalent
of a dead goat

for actions degrading our humanity
and our standing in the global community

Uncle Sam
i pin this poem on your chest
sorry for the prick
it will only bleed
a little bit

we could be heroes

the immigrant frying my fries at McDonald's is a hero
the person in customer service telling me there will be a
five dollar charge if she assists me paying my bill over
the phone is a hero
the guy using his gas engine portable leaf blower to
move his cloud of dust across the street at 7 a.m.
on a Saturday is a hero
the state policeman in New Mexico caught in broad
daylight on video doing the wham-bam-thank-you-ma'am
with his girlfriend on the hood of her car is a hero
the Bank of (screw) America exec kicking sr. citizens
out of their homes and into the streets is a hero
the man rounding up shopping carts in the Piggly Wiggly
parking lot is a hero
the homeless dude passed out on the bench at the bus stop
is a hero
the lady behind the bulletproof glass collecting my money
where i buy gas is a hero
the attendant wiping down the machines at the laundry mat
is a hero
the hooker working Central Ave. by the sports bar is a hero
the sanitation engineer mopping the floor at the
VA hospital is a hero
the salesperson selling me two pair of eyeglasses for
the price of one is a hero
the plumber unplugging my toilet is a hero
the people who don't know what a turn signal is for
are heroes
the mother shopping at Walmart with her teenage daughter
wearing bright orange Hooters' shorts is a hero
the guy who shows up to figure out why my internet is
on the blink is a hero
the goofy looking young man who owns Facebook
is a hero
the Pope protecting pedophile priests is a hero
the neighbors growing their own tomatoes are heroes
the hipster posing in patio seating at the trendy bistro

sipping a microbrew is a hero
the people at home all alone in the dark watching porn
on their computers are heroes
the pro quarterback who corners an underage girl in
the women's bathroom against her will while his pals
stand outside and block the door is a hero
the minute man racist who kills his girlfriend and then
shoots himself dead is a hero
the person with the keys to the closet where the banned
books are stored is a hero
the poet working at Starbucks with an MFA degree
in creative writing is a hero
the friend who lets the vice-president use his face
for target practice is a hero

heroes everywhere
heroes nowhere

the night Nixon landed in China

all the networks were
covering the crook's
big moment in history
his song and dance
for the cameras
the performance of
his life to convince us
that he really was
a good guy worth
remembering

and just as the steps
were pushed up against
Air Force One and the door
opened wide so we could see
his phony smile that always
seemed to be saying
"don't-you-wish-you'd-
gone-to-the-prom-with-
me-now-bitch?"

Marilyn looked at
a clock and said the
frozen pizza was done
she gave me the bong
tried to stand up
fell on her plump ass
then she started to laugh
we all started to laugh

our president was a dick
we had the munchies
someone turned off the t.v.
the pizza was very good

strange fruit

she held out her hand, offered him a bite,
cupping what looked like a plump, bruised
testicle in the soft flesh of her palm.
he politely declined, remembered the
tree in his grandma's backyard, how the fruit
would ripen and drop to the ground where the
rotting skin swelled and split in summer's
heat as guts were left sticky and exposed.
the fat, black flies would come, hover for days,
feast and vomit like decadent Romans.

but she insisted, lifted the fig to
his mouth, teased his reluctant tongue. the taste
of its sweet red meat went down easy like
oysters. he licked his lips, asked her for more.

Marilyn

it was *The Seven Year Itch* that did it
making my five-yr.-old groin turn and churn
when i saw you on t.v. it clicked on a switch
i still haven't been able to turn off
the urge to wrap my arms around
a perfect stranger and hug for all it's worth
was a strange and new thing

unlike any woman in my life
the thought of you rolling *tortillas* at dawn
and boiling a pot of beans at noon
never entered my mind

i became aware of when your movies were
scheduled to be televised and they were watched
with more interest than anything Popeye or Bugs Bunny
had to offer

and it only stands to reason that the first little girl
i cornered and kissed in the first grade was Vanessa
a pretty blonde with a great pair of gams

now, i know how Hollywood screwed with both of us
imprinted me with a fantasy of full lips, soft curves
bubble baths and silky sheets
as you were repackaged and hawked
new and improved
time and time again

but i can still remember sitting in the backseat
of the car, my mother driving and turning up the radio
when some guy on KRLA came on the air
and said that you were found dead

i looked out the window, up towards the clouds
and asked no one in particular
"who am i going to marry now?"

a sin to remember

sixty miles away from her home
making love on the sly at
the Holiday Inn with a
view of the interstate

i find and kiss secret places
she forgot existed
neglected so long they
bloom from my touch
like desert flowers in the rain
after a hundred year drought

when suddenly
sunlight from ninety-three million
miles away comes through a
thin parting between the curtains
lands on the diamond ring
she took off and placed
on the nightstand

the room explodes into
a flash of celestial fire
scorched by the heavens
and the heat of our desire

a birthday wish for a friend

here's hoping your day starts
with the alarm not going off
you oversleep until the
phone rings and it's
Keith Richards calling to
say he's got room for one
more on his yacht
a limo picks you up
whisks you off to the airport
by noon you land in L.A.
by one you're onboard
headed south along
the Mexican Riviera
you decide to sunbathe
topless wondering where
the last fifty years have
gone and how good the
sun and salt air feels
on your bare breasts
you fall asleep as the
boat rocks gently on
the ocean's waves

you wake up and find
an old man wrinkled
like a white prune with
a solid gold earring tangled
in his long unkempt grey hair
he's stretched out at your side
wearing nothing but Speedos
with a pair of giant lips and
a big red tongue on his arse
a lit cigarette dangles from
the corner of his mouth
but best of all is even though

he is asleep, he doesn't snore
which is about all you can
ask for at this age

and that's when you say to
yourself while pouring
a flute of $500-a-bottle
champagne

"Loree, this is
the best goddamn birthday
you've ever had."

why i feed the birds

once
i saw my grandmother hold out
her hand cupping a small offering
of seed to one of the wild sparrows
that frequented the bird bath she
filled with fresh water every day

she stood still
maybe stopped breathing
while the sparrow looked
at her, then the seed
then back as if he was
judging her character

he jumped into her hand
began to eat
she smiled

a woman holding
a small god

smoking outside in the alley at 3 a.m.

she yells the name of a friend
to come down and let her in
a cat locked out of the house
she calls out over and over
as the tired sound of her voice
bounces off walls of stone and
concrete then fades into a
summer night air clinging
to everything like syrup

i get up and look out
my second floor window
see bright tip of her
lit cigarette glowing
in the shadows
i imagine the faint scent
of lime and rum
the grease stained tens
and twenties stuffed
in her crevices and cracks
her limp dirty blonde
hair tangled in sweat
and Friday night cum

looking up
she sees me
looking down

she blows angry smoke into the air
asks "what the fuck is your problem?"

i gaze long at my
thrift store Barbie
knowing whatever i say
will be the wrong answer

the origami master's wife speaks

i know my true role
more servant than wife
watching how he strokes
a new piece of crisp paper
as if touching a virginal lover's
revealed skin for the first time
his fingers stroke and caress
the smooth pristine surface
while a god-like mind begins
to impose a form through
crease, bend, and fold
then setting upon it
with a creator's passion
hands in motion with
the laws of a universe
beyond my grasp

you ask why do i stay?
one winter morning
i got up before him
to start a fire and
boil water for his tea
i lit a candle and
saw my breath hang
in the air like a small
cold cloud over the
kitchen table

where i found a lone
butterfly the color
of a sunflower's bloom
perched on the lip
of my cup

his tender greeting
blowing gentle on
the dying embers
of my heart

i have Sandra's boots

the pair she wears on the original
cover of *My Wicked Wicked Ways*

bloody red lips shape into her
the-world-is-my-oyster smile

black spaghetti strap dress
pulls up high over crossed legs

an almost empty glass of merlot
stands at her dainty booted feet

boots with white stitching
criss-crossing Mexican black
leather like intricate tattoos on a
one-eyed bartender's bicep

boots that i can hear
crunching the gravel
and broken glass in
the parking lot of
a Texas cantina at
3 a.m. on a Sunday
morning and a woman's
firm *nalgas* pressing
against the door of
a rusty sky blue Chevy
pickup while the taste
of her tequila soaked
tongue tickles the
back of my throat

boots that will kick
my ass to hell and back

and make me whisper
"more"

father's day poem

you bought me a new kite
every spring and we would
go find a vacant lot or empty
field where you taught me
the intricacies of flying

how to subdue the weaving
from side to side and not
let out the string too fast
or how one hard tug makes
it jump up where it will
catch a current of wind
lifting it high and far

we stood there side
by side not saying much
but sharing a sacred moment
when knowledge is passed
on between father and son

as our kite pulled on
its string trying to
join the white billows
above

childhood's end

I. 1960
words sharp as broken
glass ornaments shredded
visions of gifts
real and imagined

"daddy didn't make a lot
of money…there won't be
a lot of presents…
there is no Santa…
and you can't tell anyone…"

she made me promise
cross my heart and hope to die
as my six-yr.-old brain
calculated the short
end of this give and take

losing something
i'd never get back as
lies, disappointment
and responsibility
took their place
under the tree

II. 1982
wondering how i got there
standing outside on a cold
December morning in front
of the Ft. Carson thrift shop
wearing a worn and ragged
red suit packed with smelly
old pillows
hiding behind a fake beard
thin and tangled
my black army boots
muddied and dull

waving at the cars passing by
i wasn't fooling anyone
a second-hand Santa
a sad lure in a business plan
right out of Marketing 101
(the-home-correspondence-course)

so i wasn't prepared
when the soldier pulled
over in his station wagon
got out and opened the
passenger door releasing
a pint-sized mob with their
short legs carrying them
as fast as they could
closing the distance between
us in small leaps and bounds

pinned under the weight of
their simple hopes and dreams
surrounded with nowhere to go
i thought of childhood's end
and promises no adult
has the right to break

i took a deep breath
picked up the smallest
of the bunch
looked her in the eye
bellowed "Merry Christmas"
like my life depended on it

her smile letting me know
no promises would be
broken today

i wouldn't wish this one on anybody

if you ever have to tell a man
his wife was raped the previous night

there is no way you can prepare
for the stare that will go right
through you like the bright
burning beam from a distant star
as it travels the speed of light

you feel your breath
sucked from the body
suddenly the realization
that doing this by yourself
might not have been
a good idea

death in the afternoon

waiting for light to change
almost miss the blackbird
swooping from my left
to my right floating across
the intersection and into
the yucca tree standing
on the edge of the corner
gas station

startled gray-brown
dove darts from yucca
as the blackbird perches
on pointed bayonet leaf
pokes head in and
brings out small gray
lump in its sharp
black beak

then
as the light changes
from red to green
it spreads shiny midnight
wings and rises up into
the turquoise sky of
the desert

living and dying, a Westside poem

snapped out of deep sleep
by the ringing sound of gun-
shots outside my window at 2 a.m.
held my breath like a deer the
split second after hearing the
crunch of dried leaves

counted minutes until the
cry of approaching sirens gave
me the ok to move about
wiped sleep from my eyes
peeked out from behind
parted curtains
watched as a beam from
a policeman's flashlight lit up
the scene

body in front seat
car doors wide open
headlights still bright
shattered glass everywhere

after running off t.v. news crews
snooping for a sound bite and
two police interviews later
i called in sick
made a pot of strong coffee
sat out front of the house and
watched the mobile crime lab
come creeping down the street
they climbed out armed with
clipboards coffee and donuts
began their routine:
took Polaroid pictures
placed plastic orange cones
by each expended shell
measured distances and angles
joked about the Dallas Cowboys
filled out some forms
interviewed me
again

they put him in a body bag

lifted it onto a gurney with
squeaky wheels and legs that
collapsed into the ass-end
of the coroner's van
a relative standing in the crowd
tried to get one last look
cursed at the officers who
held him back

the car was hauled away
by Joe's 24 Hour Towing Service
while news cameras were broken
down and loaded up
raced off to reports of local school
lock down... armed stranger...
manhunt... hysterical parents

a week later
everything is as it
should be
the trash is picked
up on Thursday and
the vendors peddle
their Mexican fruit-
flavored popsicles
from their banged up
carts

or so it seems
until i look across
the street
see the lone
bullet hole
glaring back from
my neighbor's
stucco'd wall

the governor abolishes the death penalty

for Bill Richardson

the next day during
rush hour traffic
the sun rises over the
Sandia Mountains
with a warm light
kissing the faces of
a thousand sinners
as we do the daily
commute to the job
condemned to a life
of penance 8 hrs.
at a time

but today
we are different

rising above ourselves over
the sacred red earth of the pueblos

rising above ourselves over
the cancer of vengeance

rising above bleached bones
of the deaths committed
for our false sense
of justice

and today
we have changed
we are angels
spreading our wings
in unison

rising above ourselves
into a cloudless
blue sky

why my ex-wife will go to heaven

one day you find yourself managing
a Hallmark gift shop in the San Bernardino
mall and it's busy because one of the major
holidays is approaching
those ones that bring in the big bucks
that make or break the quarterly profit report
the report that keeps the home office happy
or gives them the excuse to ride your ass into
the ground for the next three months
so this is what it comes down to
as your crew of underpaid clerks
man the register and cruise the aisles
helping customers locate that special piece
of made-in-China merchandise with a
sappy card to match

and as you take position up front to
meet and greet the crowd you notice
the young mother with her toddler in hand
you know the type well
she'll browse and take her time while
junior is turned loose to make like
a Tasmanian devil touching and grabbing
his heart's desire as your staff is transformed
into a team of impromptu babysitters
this is how it is and you accept it

a few minutes go by and you see
the child again as he is leaving the store
but this time someone else is holding his hand
someone avoiding eye contact
someone trying to walk fast and not be noticed

years later you take stock of life's ups and downs
while sitting in a bar in Rockford, Illinois, stacking
achievements and accomplishments against the failures
and the near-misses
wonder what the hell went wrong

always remember this:
how you didn't hesitate to approach them
as they attempted to leave
how you ignored the man at his side and
bent down so you looked the kid eye to eye
and asked, "where's your mommy?"
how you heard the sinister whoosh of hot air
as his hand was dropped and the faceless stranger
stepped into the crowd
vanished

later, after reports by security and interviews with police
you took a phone call from the near-hysterical parents
who kept repeating "thank you, God bless you,
thank you, God bless you, thank you, God bless you…"

they were chanting for you
elevating your spirit and
that's as good as it gets

women and guns

I.
she says she sleeps with one under her pillow
her daddy bought it for her and they
like to spend Saturday mornings walking
in the woods and shooting at shit
i know where i'm not sleeping tonight

II.
she's new in town
carrying a chip on her shoulder the size of Brooklyn
which also happens to be where she's from
while driving around in her '93 Nissan looking
for a place that's supposed to make a mean falafel
she tells me her gun is in the trunk and it's a good thing
because the way people drive in this town
if it was within reach she'd use it to blow away
the next idiot who cuts her off
i know where i'm not sleeping
ever

III.
i'm talking to my ex on the phone
about the crazy women i've been meeting lately
and she says (half joking half serious)
hell, it's good for you i didn't have one
when we were breaking up because i sure
would have used it

i hang up feeling like my luck
is about to run out

we go boom

after Patti Smith's cover of "My Generation"

they call us boomers
and we go boom
throw ourselves
on the floor
hold our breath
turn blue in the face
get our way
with our dollar
and our vote

we don't die and refuse to get old
we hold on tight and won't let go

this is mine
that's mine
those will
be mine

they call us boomers
watch us go boom
they call us boomers

boom
Boom
BOOM

the company provides free lunch on the day it lays off 250 employees

we turn off our computers at noon
carry a box with our personal items
framed family pics and employee
of the month coffee mugs
small potted plants and clock radios

we are led down the hallway
with its antiseptic floors and off-
white walls to the free lunch
they are providing before we
are shown the door one last time
some hold on to their boxes as
if they are naked and are
trying to hide their genitals

we march by the HR table
in order to pick up our severance
we must sign release papers that
prevent us from telling
others what was done to us
how it made us feel
to be blackmailed
into silence

we stand in line
we are given
one rib
one piece
of chicken
a small plastic
container of
cole slaw
one-third of
a cob of corn
a tab of butter substitute
wrapped in foil
packages of salt

and pepper (one each)
BBQ sauce also in
a small plastic cup
a roll
a cookie
one white plastic fork
and knife
a crisp neatly folded
white paper napkin

one can of soda
(off brand)

no hard feelings

we eat our "happy-
lay-off-day" lunch
as a slideshow is
projected onto a
big screen
images of past
Christmas parties
birthdays and potlucks
winners of the
annual Halloween
costume contest and
the company softball
team while a recording
of "The Way We Were"
spins on someone's
portable CD player

workers cry
go from table to
table and hug as
a few angry ones
toss the food in
the garbage and
walk out

right past the
rented security guards
stationed at each door
their eyes scanning
the room

scanning us

a goodbye

as i approach the exit
that leads to the employee
parking lot
the security guard motions
me over to his desk

a young beefed up
Scatman Carothers
head bald and shiny
a pearly-shine smile
his linebacker shoulders
wide and thick with muscle
under his white long-
sleeved shirt

for five years we've given
each other shit about the
teams we both support
Bears and Bulls for him
Lakers and Raiders for me
our bets were never
over five dollars

i walk over
prepare to shake
his hand but instead
he looks inside my box
moves my stuff around
sniffing for post-it notes
paperclips or a
coveted stapler

"sorry, man"
he says
"i gotta
do this"

once he is satisfied
i'm not stealing anything
he waves me on
i head for the door
imagine hearing
him call out
"good luck"

last day / final exit

From the driver's seat of my eleven-
yr-old Hyundai in need of an oil change
and new brakes, I wait as the gate opens.
I look into the rear view mirror. Strange
tired eyes greet me. I see crows' feet, red
where there should be white. My pepper gray beard
and love handles speak of sick days instead
of perfect attendance. HR reps steer
clear of old guys like me, prefer bodies
who prance like stallions with shiny teeth.
It's October. Autumn wind shakes the trees'
branches bare. Golden leaves rot in the street.

The army taught me words for times like this
"When you fuck me, at least give me a kiss."

the temp

walks in the room
knows the score
sees the pecking order
smells the hierarchy

hears the screams
floating in their pupils
feels hyena grins circling
behind his back

then he sits at the desk
in the corner with
the broken chair
that no one wants

turns on the computer
gets to work and hopes
they'll ask him to stay

almost bottom

out of work five months
standing at the checkout
buying a loaf of white bread
and a package of bologna
i'm paying with a pocketful
of loose change
a few quarters
a lot of dimes and nickels
a handful of pennies
stacking the change
making it easy for
the cashier to count

the line behind me
is getting longer and
i lose track of the amount
so i have to start over
feel like shit because
i've stood in that line
watching people like me
fumble with their food stamps
and jelly jars full of coins
fumed in silence while
they wasted my time

my hand is shaking
and i'm about to lose it
just walk out the door
make do with whatever
is in my cupboard
when the cashier
says "take your time
it's all right" and just
like that i calm down
and finish counting
he scoops up the change

then says
"have a nice day"

no regrets

i haven't owned a suit for over 10 yrs.
a necktie makes me turn around
and head in the other direction

my jeans are bought on sale
i wear them until the holes
in the knees get too big
my favorite t-shirt has a picture of
Thelonius Monk on the back
saying "sometimes it's to your advantage
for people to think you're crazy"
my shoes are comfortable
made for walking fast down
dark alleys or summer strolls
on sidewalks when women
put on shorts and show off
their pretty legs

i don't ride corporate jets
or company limos
the last helicopter i rode in
was at Ft. Benning
the summer of '79
when they were training us
how to jump out of one
and be prepared to shoot
something before our feet
touched the ground

i don't make those big
important decisions like
how to convince people
to buy something they
don't need while paying
them as little as possible
to make it

now
out of work
doing the unemployed shuffle
eating off the dollar menu
buying gas five bucks at a time
wondering if the good old days
are gone for good

i watch them as they tell everyone
who will listen if they go down
they're taking all of us with them
read about how they make sure
the suits are still getting bonuses
and motivational retreats at secluded
5 star hotels while eating thick cuts
of pink meat and baked potatoes
floating in hot pools of butter

today i bought a lottery ticket
my only hope for a bailout
i folded it up and put it
in my wallet

once in a while i pull it out
and hold it in my hand
as i mentally add up the
loose change in my pocket

two-coyote day at Rinconada Canyon

black rock mesa walls
eternal gift from
distant volcanoes in
quiet deep sleep

high desert sage winter-dry
brittle skeletons anchored
in ancient dirt peppered
with rabbit droppings

etched into cold hard
flat rock surface
shapes and figures of
another time when

man heard wisdom
carried on the breath
of the mesa winds

at night listened as
the stars whispered
dark stories of
the beginning
and the end

milagro #1

the green *nopales*
growing in the alley
are capped with snow
melting into cold
drops of water

bejeweling pointed
spines with pearls
fallen from the sky

milagro #2

this morning she leaves me
four strawberries on the
kitchen counter

the first strawberries
of spring

and when i bite one
its juice squirts on
my tongue sweet
like a woman's kiss
that says yes
yes and
yes

milagro #3

standing outside under
full moon circled
with eerie rings
of luminescence

neighbors celebrating
Passover with solemn
songs of long ago
when a bloodied
door kept the angel
of death at bay

their songs
chants and prayers
float over the fence
chill me to the bone

tonight i can
believe anything

milagro #4

for Lisa

squatting down
using her small
finger to poke holes
in the soft dirt

she drops seed
inside each one
covers them
with loose soil
pats it in place
with the palm of
her delicate hand

she says loudly
enough for me
to hear: when
summer comes
we will have
watermelon
and *jalapeños*

my little goddess
of the earth
grower of things
hot and sweet

my life is full
of flavor

because of you

waking up

when the rains came
we stepped outside
felt the heavy blanket
of summer heat lifted
from the blacktop and
concrete of this oven
we call a city

held each other
as the cool drops
stung our faces
rolled down the
back of our necks

i kissed her short wet
hair then let my lips
linger on the slick
skin of her brow
while wicked streaks
of electricity cracked
the night sky open
she nuzzled my neck
as a rolling thunder
shook our listless
senses awake

we went back inside
took off our
wet clothes

didn't bother to
dry off

sea turtle swimming to L.A.

it had rained hard
the day before
and the water
flowed from the city
to the ocean
a river of dirty
brown scum
a soup of
Styrofoam cups
discarded plastic bags
used condoms
dirty hypodermics
empty coke bottles
tires and super market
shopping carts

all floating to the sea
as i rode my bike
on the trail along
the top of the concrete
riverbed looking for
sun and exercise
and nature

out of the corner of my eye
i saw something surface
it was big and was swimming
against the current
poking its head
out of the water
as if trying to figure
out how much further
it had to go
i wanted to jump in
turn it around
say you're going
the wrong way

my friend
believe me that's
the last place you
want to be

but while gauging what
kind of bio hazards
i'd be exposed to
and if it was something
i really wanted to do
the turtle dived back
into the dark muck
paddling with its
flapping wing-like fins
so i continued my
ride to the beach

where i stopped at a
coffee shop in Seal Beach
ordered a latte and a scone
sat on a bench
watched the girls
baking in the sun
surrounded by signs
warning that the water
was not safe
for swimming

lowered expectations

we're watching t.v.
and a commercial comes on
it's the cuddly little cartoon
bear who squats under
a tree and uses too much
toilet paper until his mama
bear gives him a roll of
the good stuff that's soft
and absorbs more than
the competition as if
the idea of animated
Bambi rip-offs wiping their
stinky furry butts with
Charmin is going to make
us go "awwww"
go out and buy some
pronto

but this commercial is
a new one depicting the
little guy finishing his
business and being chased
down by his mom because
he's got bits of paper
(honest to god)
sticking to his behind
and she uses Charmin
to wipe off his chubby ass
a voice is telling us
how this latest improved
version doesn't leave
behind annoying paper bits
that cling and I'm thinking
"Jesus, they finally created
dingleberry-free toilet paper"

maybe i won't see world
peace in my time
but this has to account
for something

a Thanksgiving poem

the day after i get word
i'll be out of work twelve days
before Christmas and read
on the internet that the big
bonuses are back on wall street
i get a check in the mail
for a poem published
in someone's anthology

they thank me for the poem
tell me i can purchase extra copies
at half price and if i don't want
the honorarium feel free
to write "void" across the check
and return it… hint, hint

it's just enough
for a really good cigar
or a 12-pack of decent beer
enough to remind me

this is as close as i'll ever
get to making a living in
the poetry biz

and that the punches
will keep coming as long
as i keep rolling

so if it's okay
i'd like to cash that check
because sometimes
the difference between
doing something stupid
and getting locked up
for a long time
or staying alive
to write another poem

is fifteen dollars

Sonny style

i'm lying in the wet spot
drifting off into our post-coital
deep sleep when she asks
if i could re-enact any
sex scene from the movies
which one would it be

immediately the wedding
from the Godfather comes
to mind the way Santino
rendezvoused with one of
his sister's bridesmaids
didn't bother to take off
his or her clothes
just unzipped and
lifted her hips as he
pounded her against
the door standing up
using his huge salami
like a battering ram
(in the book he was
hung like a horse)

i consider my current condition
the bad back and how i can't lift
anything over 50 lbs. and
how sometimes it takes
a lot of coaxing to get
my little pony to poke
his head out of the
starting gate (don't laugh
you'll get there soon enough)

i mumble
"i love you baby"
and say goodnight

i dream

i'm sitting by myself
alone in that big place
they have in airports
where people wait for
their luggage

the sounds of moving metal
announces the first pieces
to come down the ramp and
onto the conveyor belt

but instead of oversized gym
bags with matching suitcases
i see and smell bodies
burned charcoal black
stiff as the dried branches on
a dead cottonwood tree
others are bloody raw like
strange cuts of meat not
available at your
local butcher shop
their disfigured faces
are frozen with mouths
gaped open

i know these dead
read about them every day on
the internet news and watch
t.v. news clips that only show me
the cleanup after the big bang
while sorrow and shame
cling to my throat like
a chunk of salty green-
yellow phlegm

this is my dream of witness
if you haven't had yours
brace yourself

you will
soon

i dream of tongues

i'm sitting in a bar in China
one of those drinking
establishments built
overnight to cater to
the Olympics crowd
featuring beers from all over
the globe and that damn
logo in my face wherever
i turn

i'm looking for a couple of poets
we wrote a book together and
we're meeting for the first time

i ask the bartender
if he knows them
he turns around and
grabs a manila envelope
from behind the register
drops it on the bar in
front of me

i reach inside and pull
out two copies of the book
each one has a human tongue
nailed to the cover
drained of blood
bleached and stiff

each tongue is tattooed
in black ink with the image
of a single feather
the quill is sharp and pointed
the barbs have all the minute
detail of a da Vinci sketch

whose barbaric vision is this?
to decorate the tongues of
poets with the ability
to soar above the clouds

why is it so beautiful?

i dream about remembering to forget

i am forgetting things. memories fade like old Polaroids left
in the sun. i tell a woman serving me breakfast that she
looks very pretty, and i introduce myself. she tells me she's
my wife and begins to cry. i don't know what to say. i don't
know. sentences are started but not finished as thoughts
drift off like red blossoms floating down the Ganges river.
i watch t.v. with my dog, Jack, at my side. he licks my hand
over and over. i pat his big German Rottweiler head,
say goodbye. he says he'll never leave me, no matter what
happens. my last lucid thoughts: trying to remember who
i wrote a note to, asking them to put me to sleep once and
for all when i become the equivalent of an eggplant. i hope
they don't lose that note. then i am sitting in a room with a
chair and a table. a shaft of sunlight comes through a
window and flecks of dust hang in the air as if time has
come to a standstill.

what is the dream and
what is real? am i dying
awake in my sleep?

city of the lost

after Ed Field's New York

i live in a city where the people have no shame
how else could they justify throwing their fast food
trash out the window as they drive down its hot streets
as if to say "look at me, i don't give a shit."
they leave spoiled disposable diapers tucked behind
newspaper vending machines and scattered
across Kmart parking lots
smelly calling cards to remind us they exist
and have mastered the art of procreation

the broken glass in the gutters gives the illusion of roads
decorated with jeweled glitter and precious shine
a conquistador's wet dream

La Llorona comes sweeping down
on the city from the Sandia Mts. to the east
races up and down it's streets and alleys
an ugly wind blowing litter and garbage
across the desert into Arizona

legend has it she is looking
for her long lost children

here
she has found them

milagro #7

after Jazz Deconstructed: Jazz and the Voice with Joy Harjo & Cornelius Eady, 4/25/12, Albuquerque, NM

Eady scats
and Harjo sax
riffs explode
fireworks of words
swirl around
from stage to
audience

message is
laugh
love
life

like magic
chakras glowing
again

i am shot
up into New Mexico
sky a meteorite
of jazz
a comet
of poetry
a shooting star
with a tail
of sparks streaking
through outer/
inner space

milagro #10

mountain fires
and strong winds
send smoke our way
eyes burn and a breath
becomes a gasp for air as
lungs turn into flip-
flopping goldfish
taken from their bowl
and dropped on a
hot sidewalk

at night
sliver of new moon
filtered through haze
is dark orange

the color of *chile*
ripening in the fields
just before it turns
blood red

chile moon
deadly moon
taking my breath away
the price i pay

to be smothered with
your beauty

wedding poem for Lily and Chris

so this is what it's come down to
after the invites are mailed and
the colors are picked and the brides-
maids cringe at the dresses they
have to wear but with the understanding
the only one that counts is the bride
as she walks down the aisle classy
like a Princess Diana with just a touch
of sultry Marilyn Monroe

the groom basically shows up
in his rented tux and shiny black shoes
tries to stay loose and not keel
over which sometimes is the
most important job of the day
love is pledged and "I do" is said
then a kiss to seal the deal
to loud and approving applause

it's on to the reception as spoons
tap on glasses and the couple's
first dance ever as Mr. and Mrs.
the cake is cut and bets are made
will they be civil about it or shove it
down each other's throat
the bride shows some leg as
the garter is slid down her shapely
calf and the single men jostle for
position like basketball players
during an inbound pass
then the ladies take the floor
leaping into the air like NFL
receivers making an end zone catch
coming down with the bouquet
doing the "I'm next" victory dance
later the DJ plays "Respect"
and "What I Like About You"

as everyone on the dance floor
is laughing and sweating because
today is for being happy

being happy with the hope that
man and woman can still share
their dreams and stand together
against the odds while making it in
a world that gets crazier
every time we turn on the
evening news

so tonight when we lie down in
our beds the joy we witnessed today
will take root and tomorrow
blossom with the realization

that maybe
just maybe
there is still enough love
left in this big whirling
ball of dysfunction
to go around
for the rest of us

bed bug love

long before that historical moment
when our first furry ancestor
decided to stand up for a better view
 they were cheering all our successes

their love-bites on our arms
legs and crotch evidence of
a passion we would all be lucky to
know at least once in our lifetime
as they love us the only way
they can because we haven't
figured out how to love ourselves

and despite our best
technological efforts to
eradicate them from our
lives once and for all
they keep coming back
getting cozy between
the sheets where they
adore us to no end
suck our juices

their bloated bellies
tight as little drums

milagro #12

our garden calls to me
for water and kind words
i stroke its green leaves
as i check underneath
for new blossoms or
the tiny beginnings of
a pepper or tomato

i stand amidst the wasps
combing the plants for
unwelcome six-legged
pests and watch them
land to drink from
cool beads of water
clinging to a leaf
just sprayed with
the hose in my hand

a black cricket jumps
out from the lettuce
annoyed by the shower
of water and finds a
drier place but still
cool and moist to
sit out the summer's heat

white winged butterflies
flitter from one flower
to the next in a dance
choreographed in their
genes and older than time

plant something
nurture it
then wait and
watch

everyday
new blessings
will be placed at
your feet

milagro #13

the usual dry
dirt now dark
and damp from
last night's first
rain of summer

morning sparrows
and finches in the
neighborhood trees
chatter back and
forth like loud
gossipy neighbors

create an early
morning cacophony
dispelling our need
for an alarm clock

renegade watermelon vines
snake through lettuce
run over sprouting
garlic and begin
climbing brick wall

we like to think
we are in charge
of this high desert
where we build
contain and
control

but
the birds laugh and
the vine creeps

milagro #14

for Joy

> *It's true the landscape forms the mind. If I stand here long enough I'll learn how to sing.*
> —Joy Harjo, Secrets from the Center of the World

after watering the garden
in the late afternoon
i pick out a cigar and
an ashtray and pour
cognac into a small
brandy snifter
i select a book of
poetry bought earlier
in the day to read
while sitting outside

where i light up
blow clouds of smoke
rising up into the air
watch desert spirits
take shape
then vanish

lifting the glass to my mouth
the liquor's rich flavors
soak my tongue with
the taste of vineyards
from a faraway land
as strong vapors tinted
with the essence of oak trees
tickle my nose before
i swallow its liquid
warmth

i read poetry written by
a wise and gentle warrior
(she once scolded me
for stepping on a red ant
that was headed for my
sandaled feet)
her words make me forget
the pains of my past
the uncertainty of
my future

i look around me
surrounded by my garden
i can hear the focused buzz of
bees gathering that last
bit of pollen before
the sun sets
and on the ground
by my feet is a growing
melon the size of
a baseball gathering
girth and circumference
like a small planet
being born

reading a poem aloud,
the garden and i
sing together
with one
voice

milagro #16

a meditation for Aurora, CO

last night
sitting under the stars
wondering why some
flicker on and off
while some burn bright

that's just the way it is
no need to make sense
the universe blinks an eye
we are here
it blinks again
we are gone

at anytime you or i
can turn a corner
make eye contact
with crazy as it
squeezes the trigger
splatter our brains in
mid-thought like a
misty red cloud
floating across the sky
as the sun sets

blink on
blink off

a shooting star
flares up in the night sky
then it is gone

let us weep tears of thanks
for the beauty we've seen
every waking moment

and for the beauty
we never will

milagro #17

Sunday morning
coffee and writing poetry
listening to Swiss Movement
on my stereo and during
Leroy Vinegar's "Kaftan"
Eddie Harris' sax starts
to honk all noisy and funky
a real prayer i can dig

when i hear the birds
outside getting excited
actually answering
sax tweets with their
own loud free form
response and for a brief
moment i'm engulfed
in a a mix of notes
everywhere and
nowhere
man-made and
natural

heaven
must be one big
jazz club

and all
God's angels
play

salvation

for Ray Bradbury

i was in the third grade
spending the weekend
at my Nana's when i found
my uncle's old *Playboy* magazine
laying on his bed in plain sight
i picked it up and flipped
through the pages
i knew it was supposed
to be a big deal from the way
grown-ups talked about it
but i have to tell you
i wasn't impressed
although i now had a
pretty good idea why
ladies were so soft
in certain places

the cartoons were interesting
but they weren't funny to me
and just as i was going to
put it down i came across
an illustration of a T-Rex
and since i was all about
dinosaurs i started reading
the text which turned out
to be a story about men
paying money to travel
back in time so they could
hunt the biggest baddest
meat eater ever to roam
the planet and when T-Rex
showed up some guy
got scared and ran off
stepping where he
wasn't supposed to

a squashed bug totally
changing evolution

the story struck me like
lightning and my blood
began to boil between my ears
i started looking for anything
the author had written
finding his books at the
local library as his words
and stories eased the pain
of growing up with a father
who i thought loved the needle
in his arm more than me

the next year my old man
o.d.'d and i sought comfort
in the pages of books
looking for something to step on
a bug to squash and turn back
the clock so i could start over with
my not-so-happy ten-yr.-old life

so i started to write stories
diving deeper into the
sea of words and language
until i couldn't come up for air
and that led to my
first poems

now
forty-eight yrs later
i'm still at it

and Ray,
you magnificent
storytelling S.O.B.

it's just me
apologizing
for how long it's
taken to say
thanks

fifty-something

it happened a year ago
it was festive and we joked amidst
black balloons and the usual
"too-old-to-screw-too-young-to-die"
birthday cards
i took it in stride
felt like i could do tequila
shots with death
if i had to

but now it's catching up to me
my body a vacant lot left off
the local beautification list as it
becomes a dumping ground for
ugly spots on my weathered skin

like a hardy breed of weed
hairs in various nooks and crannies
demand a weekly trim
sucking in my gut for a babe
passing by is more trouble
than it's worth and the final blow…
the new music doesn't make sense

this morning i found a white hair
where there has never been one before
pushing its way through
threatening to take over like an
epidemic of pubic crabgrass
without giving any thought to
the consequences i plucked it out
and in doing so reminded myself
what a painful process this
is going to be

something to look forward to

i'm visiting the local
senior citizen center
for the first time because
my age qualifies me to
use their brand new gym
and their 50 cents per visit
is a deal i can't pass up

the lady at the main desk
points out the way and
as i walk through the
building i see old guys
sitting alone working
on 500-piece jigsaw puzzles
and a group of elderly
dames following directions
as their young instructor
leads them through some
stretching exercises
another group of people
are sitting at tables
chatting away and eating
their sr. citizen lunch

i'm thinking "whoaaa, this is like
being back in kindergarten"
and even though the new
gym looks pretty cool
i'm going to have to
give this some thought because
coming here regularly is going
to make me feel like
i'm just a few steps away

from the last recess

funeral song

finally, bring it on home
with Joe Williams singing
"Every Day I Have the Blues"
not the big band version he sang
while fronting for Count Basie
during the 1950s
but the mellow number he did
decades later while backed
by a jazz combo in a small
club in L.A.
if your feet ain't moving
when Joe belts out about
how "I've had my share
of bad luck and trouble"
then maybe you should
be in the box instead of me
because i did have the blues
most days but learned
to deal with it and get myself
out of bed one day at a time
gave it my best shot
again and again
living and loving and crying
and laughing and fornicating
and fighting and learning
and trying and writing
and working and finally
dying

now my time is up
just let me step aside
vacate this space
so someone else
can take my place

final words

last breath on your lips,
heartbeat whispers in your ear
"it was the bacon."

RICHARD VARGAS was born in Compton, California, and attended schools in Compton, Lynwood, and Paramount. He earned his BA at Cal State University, Long Beach, where he studied under Gerald Locklin and Richard Lee, and received his MFA from the University of New Mexico. He edited and published five issues of *The Tequila Review* from 1978 to 1980. His first book, *McLife*, was featured on *The Writers Almanac with Garrison Keillor*, and a second book, *American Jesus*, was published by Tia Chucha Press (2007). Vargas was recipient of the 2011 Taos Summer Writers' Conference's Hispanic Writer Award and was on faculty at the 10th National Latino Writers Conference in 2012. Today he resides in Albuquerque, New Mexico, where he edits and publishes *The Más Tequila Review*.

Cover artist **MAHWISH CHISHTY** lives in Chicago, Illinois, and initially trained as a miniature painter from the National College of Arts in Lahore, Pakistan. She has since aggressively combined new media and conceptual work with her traditional practice. Her formal paintings depict contradictions and irony within its pictorial coding. Starting from a silhouette of UAV, she paints colorful folk 'truck art' imagery on these war machines to give them a second skin that opens a dialogue about Pakistani common culture. These paintings are accompanied by culturally loaded text and iconography to communicate phrases like:

> "Look at me but with love"
> "Honk your horn before passing me"
> And "Go in peace; Come back in peace"

These expressions in combination with stark iconography gives birth to a new visual language. Ms. Chishty's recent pieces challenge the grotesque reality of modern warfare by combining layers of photo-transferred images from Pakistani print media and tradition of miniature painting. She is interested in the contrast of terror with the representation of cultural beauty.

Ms. Chishty has exhibited her work nationally and internationally at venues like the Museum of Contemporary African Diasporan Arts (MOCADA), Brooklyn, NY; Maryland Art Place, Baltimore, MD; Gallery 10, Washington D.C., and

Rohtas Gallery, Lahore, Pakistan, among others. In November 2013, her work was featured at UTS gallery in Sydney, Australia. Ms. Chishty also has pieces in public and private collections, including the Foreign office Islamabad, Pakistan and Fukuoka Asian Art Museum, Fukuoka Shi, Japan.

www.ingramcontent.com/pod-product-compliance
Lightning Source LLC
LaVergne TN
LVHW041341080426
835512LV00006B/558